Simply Foil Grill & Oven Recipes

Make Simple, Easy, Friendly and Healthy
foil packet dinner

EMMILY COLLINE

Table of Contents

Introduction

One of the great myths about aluminum foil is that when baking with it, you always put the shiny surface of the aluminum foil on the inside and the dull surface on the outside. The dull side absorbed the heat into what you were cooking, and the shiny side reflected it back inside, keeping the heat in. In fact, however, aluminum foil has a dull side and a shiny side simply because of the way it is processed. Although the two sides of aluminum foil may look different, there is no appreciable difference in heat reflection or transmission on either side.

Foils also continues to offer a lot of benefits in home kitchen use:

- Keeps out oxygen and preserves the aroma
- Impermeable to moisture and water vapor
- Keeps out light and air
- Odorless
- Non-toxic and corrosion resistant
- Excellent conductor of heat in cooking

Foils stays wrapped around food items without needing further sealing and it is hygienic unlike plastic, it can be thoroughly cleaned.

Some people say that aluminum foil is a better choice for wrapping foods for freezer storage than plastic wrap, as it protects better from moisture loss (which causes freezer burn.) Many householders cover themselves by wrapping foods especially foods that can be delicate to freeze such as fish — first in plastic wrap, then in aluminum foil.

Foil sometimes react with highly salted or highly acidic foods, such as tomato sauces to produce aluminum salt, which is harmless, but still unsettling when your dinner guests are watching. The reaction can also create pinholes in the foil. To avoid this, use plastic wrap instead or put a layer of plastic wrap between the food and the tin foil.

No matter what time of the year, foil packet recipes are always in season. Taking the fuss out of cooking, especially when it comes to dinner recipes, foil packets can be baked, roasted, grilled, or tossed over an open campfire. Who says camping food is only hotdogs and roasted marshmallows? Simply load up the camper kitchen with your favorite flavor combinations, make sure the packs are completely sealed, cook, and enjoy some campfire meals. When cooking your foil packet meal, be sure to use a heavy duty aluminum foil. This will prevent tearing and the wonderful juices from oozing out of your meal.

When in doubt, you can always double up on foil, especially when you boil foil packets.

When you package your foods with aluminum foil you are avoiding a large number bacterias that could end up floating around in your home cooked meals. Although there are a few disadvantages to using foil compared to other packaging products, the advantages truly out weigh the negatives. Before deciding on whether or not you want to use foil or plastic, be sure to look for the pros and cons of each product before you make your purchase. Below you will find a list of great advantages to using aluminum foil to package your foods.

Packaging your food with aluminum foil will help prevent the food from coming in contact with germs, as it is highly resistant to all bacterias. Because aluminum foil can be easily torn, add an extra layer to your packaging to insure yourself that nothing will come into contact with the food.

Did you know you could do this with foil? This easy cooking technique makes flavorful dinners on the grill—or in the oven—all while making clean-up a breeze!

We have a great collection of wrap-and-cook foil packet recipes, but you can make almost anything in aluminum foil. This book will teach you everything you need to know about making these prep-ahead meals.

CAULIFLOWER CURRY

Cauliflower Curry Grill Packets are as fun to make, as they are to eat! This delicious vegan and gluten-free recipe is from Vegan Yack Attack on the Go. These Vegan grill foil packets are loaded with flavor and perfect for summer parties. This vegetable-loaded meal hardly compromises taste thanks to its light curry and yogurt sauce additions. It is so good; your family will have no idea how healthy it actually is.

PREP TIME: 15 minutes

COOK TIME: 15 minutes

TOTAL TIME: 30 minutes

Cauliflower Curry

Ingredients

For the yogurt sauce:

- 1 cup of plain nondairy yogurt

- 2 tablespoons of chopped cilantro

- 2 tablespoons of thinly sliced scallions

- 1 tablespoon of lime juice

- ½ teaspoon of onion powder

- ½ teaspoon of lime zest

- ¼ teaspoon of salt

For the curry cauliflower:

- 1 pound of cauliflower florets chopped into bite-sized pieces

- 1 pound of russet potatoes diced

- 1 cup of chopped white onion

- 1 cup of halved cherry tomatoes

- 1 cup of green peas

- 1 can chickpeas drained and rinsed (15 ounces)

- 1½ tablespoons of melted coconut oil

- 1½ tablespoons of curry powder

- Pinch of salt

- Dash of pepper
- 1 tablespoon of lemon juice

Preparation

To make the yogurt sauce:

1. Place all the yogurt sauce ingredients in a small mixing bowl, and stir until combined.
2. Refrigerate until ready to serve.

To make the curry cauliflower:

1. Preheat the grill to roughly 400ºF (204ºC).
2. Place the cauliflower, potatoes, white onions, tomatoes, peas, and chickpeas in a very large mixing bowl.
3. Drizzle the coconut oil over the top of the veggies, and stir very well until it is well coated.
4. Add the curry powder and a pinch of salt and pepper, and stir again until evenly coated.
5. Tear out 4 pieces of aluminum foil that are 12 x 18 inches (30 x 46 cm), and lay them out.
6. Divide the curry cauliflower mixture between the 4 sheets, place it in the middle.
7. Fold the two long sides in toward the middle, and fold the seam together until it hits the filling.

8. Fold the two short sides in, twice, to seal the ends.

9. Place each packet on the grill and cook for 7 minutes, flip them over and grill for an additional 7 minutes.

10. Carefully, open one packet slightly, and poke the cauliflower and potatoes to see if they are Soft. If not, cook until they are.

11. Once it is cooked through, place the packets on a cooling rack for 5 minutes before opening and serving.

12. When the packets are opened, squeeze lemon juice over each one, and top with salt and pepper.

13. Serve the packets alongside yogurt sauce and enjoy.

CHICKEN CORDON BLEU

Busy night ahead of you? Make putting dinner on the table the least of your concerns with these ham, chicken, and potato-infused packets, which only require 10 minutes of prep and 20 minutes of cooking. They are easy to prep ahead and make a great camping meal, can be cooked on the grill or in the oven. It is a true one "pack" meal.

PREP TIME: 10 minutes

COOK TIME: 20 minutes

TOTAL TIME: 30 minutes

Chicken Cordon Bleu

Ingredients

- 2 boneless, skinless chicken breasts cubed
- 300 grams of Little Potatoes about 16-20, halved
- 1 cup of cooked ham cubed
- 2 tablespoons of canola oil
- 1 teaspoon of seasoning salt
- 1 teaspoon of Italian seasoning
- ¼ teaspoon of dry mustard
- ¼ teaspoon of black pepper
- 1 cup of shredded Swiss cheese

Preparation

1. Preheat the grill to medium-high, or about 400 degrees F.
2. Combine all ingredients except for the cheese, in a large bowl, (chicken through pepper).
3. Stir very well.
4. Lay one piece of tin foil on top of another and spray the center lightly with nonstick spray.
5. Spoon ¼ of the chicken mixture into the center of the foil, and fold to seal completely.

6. Grill over direct heat for about 20 minutes, until a meat thermometer inserted in the thickest piece of chicken reaches 165 degrees F.

7. Open packets and sprinkle each with ¼ cup of cheese.

8. Close the grill for 2-3 minutes, just until melted.

9. Serve and enjoy.

PHILLY CHEESE STEAK

Take the mess out of eating this classic meal by mixing the sandwich rolls and digging in the classy way with a fork. Perfect for the campfire, grill, or the oven!

PREP TIME: 15 minutes

COOK TIME: 20 minutes

TOTAL TIME: 35 minutes

Philly Cheese Steak

Ingredients

- Heavy Duty Foil
- 2 large (1/2 Pound) Yukon Gold potatoes, chopped into bite-sized pieces
- 1 large green pepper, chopped into bite-sized pieces
- 1/2 cup of yellow onion, diced
- 6 ounces (1 cup) brown sliced mushrooms
- 3 tablespoons of olive oil
- 1 Pound of lean grinded beef (95/5 or 93/7 mix)
- 1 tablespoon of Worcestershire sauce
- 2 tablespoons of ketchup
- 1/2 teaspoon of each: paprika, onion powder, garlic powder
- 1/4 teaspoon of cayenne pepper
- 1 ½ teaspoons of Italian seasoning
- Fine sea salt and freshly cracked pepper
- 6 slices of provolone cheese

Preparation

If using a grill:

1. Preheat to 525-550 degrees F

13

If using an oven

2. Preheat to 400 degrees F.

3. Set out 4 large sheets of heavy duty foil.

Prep the veggies:

4. Scrub the potatoes clean and dry them.

5. Cut the potatoes into bite-sized pieces.

6. Cut the green pepper into bite-sized pieces (discard seeds and ribs).

7. Dice the yellow onion.

8. Slice the mushrooms.

9. Add all these veggies to a large bowl and add the olive oil, and salt + pepper to taste (1 ½ teaspoon of salt and ¼ teaspoon of pepper).

10. Toss to completely coat all the veggies and then evenly disperse this mixture among the prepared foil.

11. In that same bowl used for the veggies (less dishes right!) add the Pound of grinded beef.

12. Add the Worcestershire sauce, ketchup, paprika, onion powder, garlic powder, cayenne pepper, Italian seasoning, salt and pepper (to taste).

13. Knead the ingredients together until well combined.

14. Separate the meat mixture evenly into 4 parts (if using a food scale, 4 ounces per portion).

15. Coarsely break each part of beef over the veggies in each foil packet.

16. Seal the foil packets making sure to leave some room for air circulation in each packet.

17. **TO GRILL:** place the packets in the middle of the grill and cook at high temperature for 10 minutes.

18. Flip the foil packets upside down and cook for another 5-10 minutes or until veggies are Soft.

19. **TO BAKE:** place the packets on a large sheet pan lined with foil (juices will leak out of the packets so make sure to really line that sheet pan for easy clean up).

20. Place the packets on and bake for 20 minutes.

21. Flip the packets and bake for 10-15 minutes more.

22. Remove foil packs from heat and carefully open the packets (watch out for the release of steam.)

GARLIC SHRIMP WITH VEGGIE

Zucchini and a handful of other veggies put a summery spin on this low-carb seafood foil packet recipe. Pair with a seasonal salad for even more festive fare. These shrimp foil packs are great for healthy eating. They are flavorful, low-carb and can be customized to make it a complete meal. For the veggies, we used zucchini but just about any other veggie would work well. Asparagus, broccoli, bell peppers, and green beans are all great options.

PREP TIME: 10 minutes

COOK TIME: 15 minutes

TOTAL TIME: 25 minutes

Garlic Shrimp With Veggie

Ingredients

- 1 pound of large shrimp peeled and deveined
- 3-4 cups of chopped zucchini or your favorite vegetables
- 4 cloves of minced garlic
- 2 tablespoons of minced cilantro or parsley
- 3 tablespoons of olive oil
- 1 teaspoon of paprika
- Salt and Pepper

Preparation

1. Add all the ingredients to a large bowl.
2. Mix to combine.
3. Place four 18x12-inch pieces of heavy aluminum foil on counter.
4. Place the shrimp and veggie mixture on the foil.
5. Fold the foil over the shrimp to seal.
6. Grill or bake at 400 degrees for 15-20 minutes or until shrimp and vegetables are cooked through.
7. Serve with rice, bread or salad.

TERIYAKI BEEF

Good luck sticking to just one of these juicy beef packets, loaded with broccoli, bell peppers, mushrooms, and potatoes. Teriyaki Beef Foil Packets – made with Soft steak, broccoli, bell peppers, mushrooms, and potatoes tossed in a sweet and savory Asian-inspired sauce. These bake up perfectly in the oven on a busy weeknight – or toss them on the grill for a weekend summer cookout.

PREP TIME: 15 minutes

COOK TIME: 15 minutes

TOTAL TIME: 30 minutes

Teriyaki Beef

Ingredients

- ½ pound of Rib-eye steak cut into 1 ½ " pieces can also use T-bone, Filet Mignon or strip steak
- Sea salt and freshly grinded black pepper to taste
- ½ of Soy Vay's Veri Veri Teriyaki Marinade and Sauce divided (can substitute with gluten free tamari or coconut aminos for paleo-friendly version)
- 1/3 cup of sliced mushrooms
- 1 cup of potatoes cut into 1 - 1 ½ " chunks, baby Yukon or baby red potatoes would work as well
- 1 small red bell pepper chopped
- 1 cup of broccoli florets
- freshly chopped parsley for topping

Preparation

1. Preheat grill to medium-high or oven to 450°F.
2. Season steak with salt, pepper and 3 Tablespoons of Soy Vay's Veri Veri Teriyaki Marinade and Sauce.
3. Add the mushrooms, potatoes, broccoli and bell peppers in a large bowl.

4. Add sesame oil and remaining Soy Vay's Veri Veri Teriyaki Marinade and Sauce and toss to combine.

5. Gently stir in the steak.

6. Cut four 18 x 12 inch squares of foil and divide the mixture evenly among each packet.

7. Fold the foil over the steak and seal to close off the packets.

8. **If cooking on the Grill:** Place foil packets onto the grill and close the lid.

9. Grill for 12 minutes, then flip over and grill for an additional 7-8 minutes.

10. Remove from heat and wait for 10 minutes, for the potatoes to steam.

11. Sprinkle with fresh parsley and additional black pepper, if desired.

12. **If cooking in the Oven:** Place foil packets on a baking sheet and cook for 18 minutes (rotating tray once).

13. Open foil packets then return to oven and turn to broil.

14. Cook for an additional 2-3 minutes, or until steak is slightly charred.

15. Remove the baking sheet from oven.

16. Seal the packets again and wait for an additional 6-8 minutes so the potatoes continue to steam and cook.

17. Sprinkle with fresh parsley and additional black pepper, if desired.

18. Serve and enjoy!

ZUCCHINI PARSEMAN

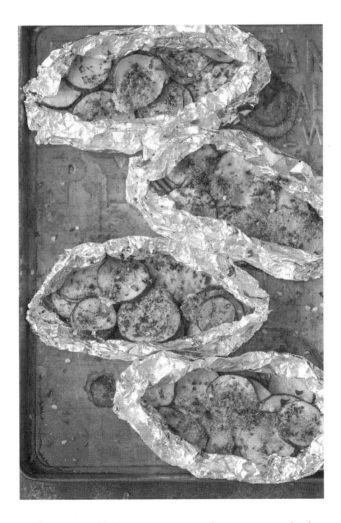

There is no shortage of light, yummy meals to serve with cheesy grilled zucchinis, meaning you can bust out this easy recipe all summer long.

Minimum effort, zero clean up and easy serving! These can also be grilled or baked so you can have it anytime, anywhere!

PREP TIME: 15 minutes

COOK TIME: 15 minutes

TOTAL TIME: 30 minutes

Zucchini Parseman

Ingredients

- ¼ cup of unsalted butter, melted
- ¼ cup of freshly grated Parmesan
- 1 teaspoon of dried basil
- 1 teaspoon of dried oregano
- Kosher salt and freshly grinded black pepper, to taste
- 4 zucchini, cut into 1/4-inch thick rounds
- ¼ teaspoon of crushed red pepper flakes
- 2 tablespoons of chopped fresh parsley leaves

Preparation

1. Preheat a gas or charcoal grill over high heat.
2. Whisk together butter, Parmesan, basil and oregano
3. Season with salt and pepper, to taste.
4. Center zucchini on a sheet of Reynolds Wrap Heavy Duty Foil.
5. Spoon the butter mixture over zucchini.
6. Bring up foil sides.
7. Double fold top and ends to seal packet, leaving room for heat circulation inside.

8. Place foil packets on the grill and cook until just cooked through, about 15-20 minutes.

9. Serve immediately, garnished with red pepper flakes and parsley, if desired.

BACON RANCH CHICKEN

Satisfy picky little eaters with this savory foil packet dinner, which you can make in just an hour. These bacon ranch chicken foil packets are a super easy dinner option with minimal cleanup! Chicken breasts are cooked with potatoes and ranch-flavored butter, and then topped with melted cheese and bacon for a meal that is sure to please any crowd.

PREP TIME: 15 minutes

COOK TIME: 45 minutes

TOTAL TIME: 1 hou

Bacon Ranch Chicken

Ingredients

- 6 tablespoons of butter melted
- 2 tablespoons of ranch seasoning powder
- Salt and Pepper to taste
- 4 medium sized chicken breasts approximately 4 ounces each
- 1 pound of small red potatoes halved or quartered
- Nonstick cooking spray
- 1 cup of shredded cheddar cheese
- 4 slices bacon cooked and crumbled
- 2 tablespoons of chopped parsley

Preparation

1. Preheat the oven to 425 degrees or a grill over medium high heat.
2. In a small bowl whisk together the butter, ranch seasoning, and salt and pepper to taste.
3. Coat 4 large squares of foil with cooking spray.
4. Place the potatoes in a bowl and drizzle with 4 tablespoons of the ranch butter over the top.
5. Toss to coat evenly.

6. Place a chicken breast onto each of the foil squares and season with salt and pepper to taste.

7. Divide the potatoes evenly among the 4 foil squares and arrange them around the chicken.

8. Drizzle the remaining 2 Tablespoons of butter over the chicken breasts.

9. Fold the edges of the foil over the chicken and potatoes to make a packet.

10. Bake for 45 minutes or grill for 30 minutes.

11. Open the packets and sprinkle the cheese over the chicken and potatoes.

12. Leave the packets open and return to the oven or grill for 2-3 minutes or until cheese melts.

13. Sprinkle with bacon and parsley and serve.

STEAK FAJITA

Ditch the tortillas and chow down on marinated steak, peppers, and onions straight from the oven-friendly packet. Soft, flavorful, and easy

Chili Lime Steak Fajitas prepared in foil packs! This no fuss, fresh and seriously delicious steak fajitas recipe is sure to be a major hit!

PREP TIME: 20 minutes

COOK TIME: 15 minutes

TOTAL TIME: 25 minutes

Steak Fajita

Ingredients

For The Marinade

- 1 Pound of flank steak, thinly sliced
- 2 juiced limes
- 2 tablespoons of olive oil
- 3 cloves garlic, minced
- ½ teaspoon of cumin
- 1 teaspoon of chili powder
- 1 teaspoon of salt

For The Fajitas

- 2 to 3 bell peppers, all different colors, sliced
- 1 medium yellow onion, sliced
- 2 teaspoons of olive oil
- ½ teaspoon of dried oregano
- ¼ teaspoon of garlic powder, or to taste
- ¼ teaspoon of sweet or smoked paprika, or to taste
- Salt and fresh grinded pepper, to taste

OPTIONAL SIDES

- Flour tortillas

- Avocado slices

- Lime wedges

- Sour cream

- Cilantro

Preparation

1. Preheat oven to 425F.

2. Place the steak slices in a large mixing bowl, a baking dish, or a freezer bag.

3. Whisk together the lime juice, olive oil, garlic, cumin, chili powder, and salt.

4. Pour the marinade over the steak slices, mix around until evenly coated, and cover.

5. Refrigerate for 15 minutes, or up to 24 hours.

6. Remove steak from fridge and leave it at room temperature.

7. Cut up four 12 x 12 aluminum foil sheets.

8. Place bell pepper slices and onion slices in a large mixing bowl and season with olive oil, oregano, garlic powder, paprika, salt and pepper stir very well to combine.

9. Portion out the peppers mixture and arrange in the center of each foil sheet.

10. Remove steak from marinade; portion out the steak slices and arrange over the vegetables inside the foil packs.

11. Discard marinade.

12. Close the foils and wrap them up tightly around the steak and vegetables.

13. Arrange foil packs on a baking sheet and cook for 15 minutes, or until done.

14. You can also grill the steak fajitas foil packets over high heat for around 7 minutes per side.

15. An instant read thermometer should read 120F in center for medium rare, and 130F for medium.

16. Remove from oven or grill.

17. Serve immediately over flour tortillas, with avocado slices, lime wedges, sour cream, and cilantro.

18. If you are on a low carb diet, serve the steak fajitas over a salad, or make lettuce wraps.

19. You can also eat this as is, straight from the foil packet.

CHESSY POTATOES

A cheese and potato combo alone is a major dinner side dish win-win, but the mess-free foil cooking method makes this recipe even more of a must. Easy and delicious side dish that can be baked in the oven or cooked on the grill! No-mess clean up makes these perfect for a quick dinner!

PREP TIME: 10 minutes

COOK TIME: 20 minutes

TOTAL TIME: 30 minutes

Chessy Potatoes

Ingredients

- 4 medium Russet or Idaho potatoes
- 4 tablespoon of unsalted butter
- 4 tablespoon of extra virgin olive oil
- ½ medium sweet onion chopped
- ¼ cup of shredded sharp cheddar cheese
- ¼ cup of shredded mozzarella cheese
- ½ teaspoon of kosher salt
- ¼ teaspoon of grinded black pepper
- ½ teaspoon of dried dill *optional*

Preparation

1. Prepare 4 sheets 12" x 10" of aluminum foil.
2. Peel and dice potatoes.
3. Place one diced potato per sheet of foil.
4. Add one tablespoon of diced onion.
5. Place one tablespoon of butter on top of potatoes and drizzle one tablespoon of olive oil.
6. Season potatoes with salt and pepper.

7. Bring the longer sides of foil sheet together and make a couple of 1" folds to close.

8. Make sure to leave enough room for the steam.

9. Close tightly the shorter sides.

10. Place foil packets on a large baking sheet.

11. **If baking in the oven:** preheat to 375 degrees F.

12. Place the baking sheet in the oven and bake for 18 to 20 minutes.

13. Carefully, open the pockets and allow steam to escape.

14. Check if potatoes are soft.

15. Sprinkle shredded cheese, dividing evenly over all pockets.

16. Scrunch down the sides of foil and place sheet back in the oven to melt the cheese.

17. You can broil them for 2 minutes, if desired.

18. **If cooking on the grill:** preheat grill to medium heat.

19. Place foil packs on the grill, close and cook for 10 minutes.

20. Flip over and cook for 10 more minutes.

21. Carefully open packs and allow steam to escape.

22. Check if potatoes are done.

23. Top with cheese and close packs for few more minutes to melt the cheese, and serve.

ITALIAN SAUSAGE AND VEGGIE

Fire up the grill and set your outdoor table, because this nutritious foil packet meal makes for the ideal al fresco family dinner. A great outdoor grill or camping recipe.

PREP TIME: 20 minutes

COOK TIME: 35 minutes

TOTAL TIME: 55 minutes

Italian Suasage And Veggie

Ingredients

- Foil Packs
- Heavy Duty Foil
- 16 ounces Smoked Italian Turkey or Chicken Sausage, coined
- 2 cups of baby red potatoes, quartered
- ¾ cup of yellow onion, diced
- 1/2 cup of cremini mushrooms, diced
- 3 small (or 2 large) bell peppers
- 4 cloves garlic, *optional*
- 4 ½ tablespoons of olive oil
- ½ tablespoon for each: dried basil, dried oregano, dried parsley, garlic powder
- ½ teaspoon for each: onion powder, dried thyme
- 1/8 teaspoon of red pepper flakes optional
- 1/3 cup of Parmesan cheese freshly grated, optional
- *Optional:* fresh parsley, salt and pepper

Preparation

1. **If using the OVEN;** preheat the oven to 425 degrees F.

2. **If GRILLING,** prepare the grill by heating to medium-high heat.

3. Prepare 4-6 large sheets of heavy duty foil; lightly spritz with cooking spray.

4. **Prep the ingredients:** wash and dry the veggies.

5. Coin the sausage.

6. Slice the baby red potatoes in half and then half again.

7. Dice the onion and mushrooms.

8. Remove the stem and seeds on the bell peppers and thinly slice.

9. Add the sausage, veggies, and garlic to a large bowl.

10. Toss with the olive oil and all of the seasonings (basil, oregano, parsley, onion powder, thyme, red pepper flakes, and a generous sprinkle of salt + pepper if desired).

11. Toss until well combined.

12. Divide the mixture evenly among the prepared sheets of foil or prepared baking pan.

13. Try to make sure 1 clove of garlic gets into each foil pack

14. Seal the foil packs tightly so no air escapes, but do not double up foil

15. **GRILL:** Grill for 25-30 minutes or until veggies have reached desired Softness

16. **BAKE in foil packs:** Bake for 30-40 minutes (at 30 minutes, veggies are crisp; 35 is perfect for us; 40 is very Soft veggies).

17. You can set the foil packs right on the oven rack or on a sheet pan for easier removal from the oven.

18. **BAKE ON SHEET PAN:** Bake for about 30-35 minutes, flipping/stirring the ingredients once at the halfway point.

19. Carefully open the foil pack expecting steam to be released.

20. Remove the garlic cloves and discard.

21. Garnish if desired with fresh chopped parsley, any additional salt/pepper, and freshly grated Parmesan cheese.

22. Enjoy immediately!

NACHO FOIL PACKET

You do not even need to bust out a bowl or serving platter—just wait for this mouthwatering appetizer to cool down from the oven and dive straight in. The Best Nachos Recipe is one that is easy, delicious, and quick. That is exactly what these Foil Packet Nachos are! Loaded with beef, tomatoes, green chiles (and more), and covered in melty cheese. These nachos can be made in the oven or on the grill.

PREP TIME: 10 minutes

COOK TIME: 15 minutes

TOTAL TIME: 25 minutes

Nacho Foil Packet

Ingredients

- 5 cups of tortilla chips
- ½ Pound of lean grinded beef
- 1.1-ounce packet Old El Paso Taco Seasoning
- 1 4.5 ounce can Old El Paso Green Chiles, drained
- ½ 14.5 ounce can diced tomatoes, fully drained
- ½ 14.5 ounce can black beans, drained and rinsed
- ½ cup of diced onion green, red, or white - whichever you love best!
- 2 cups of Mexican blend cheese
- ½ cup of fresh cilantro finely chopped
- Sour cream for garnish

Preparation

1. Heat grill to medium high heat (or heat oven to 350F)
2. In a large skillet, brown beef over medium high heat.
3. Stir in the taco seasoning and stir to coat.
4. When almost browned, toss in the tomatoes and green chiles (both fully drained) and stir to combine.
5. Remove from heat and set aside.

6. Fold two large 12x24 inch sheets of foil in half and fold up the edges to create the bottom of each packet.

7. If you prefer smaller packets, you can use 12x12 inch pieces and divide ingredients into fourths instead of halves.

8. Place half the chips at the bottom of each foil packet.

9. Sprinkle each with half the beef mixture, half the black beans, half the onion, and top with half the cheese.

10. Lastly sprinkle with chopped cilantro.

11. Fold the other half of each foil packet and pinch shut.

12. Cut a hole in the top of each packet as shown so steam can vent (and avoid chips getting too soggy).

13. Bake or grill for 12-15 minutes or until cheese is fully melted.

14. Top with sour cream, jalapenos, or your fave nacho toppings.

15. Enjoy!

GRILLED PINEAPPLE CHICKEN

Teriyaki sauce and Asian toasted sesame dressing pack a flavorful punch with this simple and satisfying five-ingredient weeknight dinner. Grilled Pineapple Chicken Foil Packets – chicken, pineapple, peppers, and onions slathered in a sweet and savory teriyaki sauce and cooked on the grill!

PREP TIME: 10 minutes

COOK TIME: 20 minutes

TOTAL TIME: 30 minutes

Grilled Pineapple Chicken

Ingredients

- 4 boneless skinless chicken breasts, cut into 1 1/2 inch pieces
- 1 red bell pepper, chopped
- 1 green bell pepper, chopped
- 1 small onion, chopped
- 1 15-ounce can pineapple chunks

Sauce

- 1 cup of teriyaki sauce
- 1 cup of Asian toasted sesame dressing

Preparation

1. Preheat the grill.
2. Lay out 4 large (about 24 inches long) pieces of foil.
3. In a bowl whisk together teriyaki sauce and sesame dressing.
4. Distribute chicken, peppers, onions, pineapple chunks, and sauce between the sheets of foil.
5. Fold the sides of the foil over the fillings and seal shut.

6. Grill packets for about 10-15 minutes, turning over once half way through. Carefully unfold foil packets and check chicken to make sure it is cooked through.

7. Garnish with cilantro and sesame seeds if desired

8. Serve immediately.

CAJUN SHRIMP

Enjoy grilled corn as if you have never tasted it before—with shrimp, red potatoes, and a fiery Cajun kick. Cajun Shrimp Foil Packets are a summer grilling favorite! We cannot get enough of the Cajun flavors with the shrimp, grilled corn, and sausage. In addition, there is NO MESS!

PREP TIME: 10 minutes

COOK TIME: 35 minutes

TOTAL TIME: 45 minutes

Cajun Shrimp

Ingredients

- 18 pieces corn on the cob (6 full cobs cut in half or in thirds)
- 4 red potatoes washed and cubed
- 25 uncooked shrimp peeled or not, it's up to you
- 1 Pound of smoked sausage cut into chunks
- ½ cup of melted butter or olive oil, to taste
- ½ cup of chicken broth you may not need that much
- 1 Tablespoon of Cajun/Creole seasoning we like to use Tony Chachere's brand, to taste
- Salt and Pepper to taste

More ingredients to try in a foil packet (optional, and to your taste)

- Italian sausage
- Chicken (cut in bite size pieces)
- Bell peppers
- Mushrooms
- Red onions
- Celery
- Carrots

Preparation

1. Heat grill to 400-degrees.

2. You can do this in your oven at the same temperature.

3. Evenly distribute corn, potatoes, shrimp, and sausage between 4 heavy-duty foil sheets (approximately 12x18 inches each).

4. Drizzle melted butter and about 2 tablespoons of chicken broth over each foil packet.

5. Season evenly and generously, to taste, with Cajun seasoning, salt, and pepper.

6. Tightly seal foil packets by folding up the sides over the contents and tightly folding up the ends over the seam.

7. Grill for 30-40 minutes or until potatoes are Soft, flipping once half-way through

8. Be careful opening the packets to check for doneness, the steam inside is very hot!

TATER TOT MEATBALL

Tater tots and meatballs and cheese, oh my! It does the trick for those easygoing Friday nights when your kids deserve to munch on something fun. This easy foil packet dinner idea is amazing because it is an entire meal with easy clean up in the foil packet! They have juicy meatballs, crisp tater tots, vegetables and of course cheese for an entire meal in a foil packet!

PREP TIME: 10 minutes

COOK TIME: 30 minutes

TOTAL TIME: 40 minutes

Tater Tot Meatball

Ingredients

- 24 ounces of Home-style meatballs Frozen
- 16 ounces of mixed vegetables Frozen
- 32 ounces of Tater Tots Frozen
- 2 teaspoon of seasoned salt
- 1 cup sharp cheddar cheese

Preparation

1. Preheat the grill or oven to 350 degrees or prepare campfire.
2. In a bowl, mix all ingredients.
3. Measure out eight 8" x 12" pieces of heavy-duty aluminum foil and spray with nonstick spray.
4. Divide the mixture between the eight foil sheets.
5. Fold each piece of foil up into a pack.
6. Fold two opposing sides together and then crimp the edges closed.
7. Double wrap if you don't have heavy duty aluminum foil.
8. Set the packets directly on the grill or in the oven on a sheet pan and cook for 30 minutes or until everything is warmed through.
9. You can also cook these over your campfire on a grate.
10. Serve immediately.

SOUTHWESTERN CHICKEN

Douse chicken breasts in salsa and cheese for a delicious spin on chicken parm. Layer the foil pack with corn to start, then top the meat with sour cream and avocado once the packet's finished grilling. These Southwestern Chicken Packets are an easy and delicious no-fuss dinner recipe you can cook with a fire (while camping), on a grill, or in an oven.

PREP TIME: 10 minutes

COOK TIME: 30 minutes

TOTAL TIME: 40 minutes

Southwestern Chicken

Ingredients

- 1 cup of frozen corn
- 1 (15ounces of) can black beans, drained and rinsed
- 1 teaspoon of taco seasoning
- 2 chicken breasts or 4 chicken softs
- salt and pepper to taste
- ½ cup of salsa or pico de gallo
- 1 cup of shredded pepper jack cheese
- Cilantro, to garnish
- Sour cream, optional
- Avocado, mashed, *optional*

Preparation

1. Pull off 4 sheets of heavy-duty tin foil (8-10 inches) and layer to create 2 packets. Lightly mist with cooking spray.
2. Stir together the corn, black beans, and taco seasoning.
3. Divide between the 2 foil packets.
4. Season the chicken with salt and pepper.
5. Place 1 chicken breast or 2 chicken Softs in each packet.
6. Top the chicken with salsa and shredded cheese.

7. Bring the two longer edges of the foil together above the food.

8. Fold the edges down twice, creating the top seal.

9. Press the side edges together and fold, creating a secure packet.

10. Cook on hot coals, a gas grill, or in a 375-degree oven for 30 to 45 minutes until chicken is cooked through.

11. Top with fresh cilantro, sour cream, and avocado before serving.

12. Serve and enjoy!

BAKED TILAPIA

Meet your healthy seafood saving grace, which takes just 15 minutes. You can also top your tilapia filets with any type of pesto or a Tablespoon of your favorite seasoning mixed with two Tablespoons of melted butter. Make a different flavor for everyone at once!

PREP TIME: 5 minutes

COOK TIME: 10 minutes

TOTAL TIME: 15 minutes

Baked Tilapia

Ingredients

- 4 tilapia filets
- kosher salt & freshly grinded black pepper
- 8 garlic cloves, minced
- 12 pats of butter, about 1/2 cup of
- 8 lemon slices
- 1 Pound of thin asparagus stalks, cut into thirds
- 12 ounces cherry tomatoes, halved

Preparation

1. Preheat oven to 400F (or preheat grill to medium).
2. Place each tilapia filet on a piece of tinfoil large enough to fold and enclose tightly.
3. Season each filet with salt and pepper.
4. Divide remaining ingredients by four.
5. Top tilapia filets with garlic, then butter and lemon slices.
6. Add asparagus and tomatoes to packets, then seal packets tightly
7. Place the packets on grill or on a baking sheet in the oven.

8. Bake for 10 minutes or until tilapia is cooked through and flakes easily with a fork.

9. Serve in foil packets or remove and place on serving plates.

10. Serve immediately.

HAWAIIAN BARBECUE CHICKEN

There is no better Time than summer to bring an island-inspired vibe to your meals. Save this for your next outdoor party, or wow your family with the tangy foil packets for dinner. Grilled Hawaiian

Barbecue Chicken in Foil has the most amazing sweet and tangy pineapple barbecue sauce! It grills to perfection with sweet pineapple and delicious summer veggies!

PREP TIME: 5 minutes

COOK TIME: 10 minutes

TOTAL TIME: 15 minutes

Hawaiian Barbecue Chicken

Ingredients

- 4 boneless skinless chicken breasts
- 1 cup of bbq sauce
- 1 15-ounce can pineapple slices *(including juice)*
- 2 teaspoons of soy sauce
- 1 teaspoon of garlic
- 1 red bell pepper, cut into cubes — *change to sweet onion*
- 2 medium zucchini, sliced
- Green onions, for garnish

Preparation

1. Heat grill to medium heat.
2. Cut 4 sheets, enough to wrap the chicken and veggies, of heavy duty foil.
3. Place chicken on the center of aluminum foil, divide the veggies, and add 2-3 pineapple slices into each packet.
4. In a bowl, whisk together bbq sauce, juice from the can of pineapple slices, soy sauce, and garlic.
5. Spread about 2 Tablespoons of the sauce on the chicken and make sure to reserve about ¼ cup.

6. Place the chicken packets onto grill and grill for 13-15 minutes flipping at about 7 minutes.

7. To serve carefully open packets, baste with reserve sauce and garnish with green onions.

8. Serve and enjoy.

HAMBURGER AND POTATO

Relive your camping glory days with the original foil packet meal—

hamburger patties. Keep it old school and cook them by the campfire,

or let them bake in the oven. Hobo Dinner Foil Packets are so simple

to make and everyone raves about them! Comforting veggies including potatoes, carrots and onions are topped with a seasoned hamburger patty and grilled or baked to Soft perfection.

PREP TIME: 15 minutes

COOK TIME: 45 minutes

TOTAL TIME: 1 hour

Hawaiian Barbecue Chicken

Ingredients

- 1 pound of lean grinded beef
- 1 package of dry onion soup mix
- 4 small potatoes peeled and sliced
- 2 cups of carrots chopped
- 1 large or 2 small onions, sliced
- 2 tablespoons of olive oil
- 1 teaspoon of garlic powder
- Salt & pepper to taste
- Condensed mushroom soup

Preparation

1. Preheat oven to 375 degrees F.
2. Combine grinded beef and dry soup mix in a bowl.
3. Form into four patties and set aside.
4. In a large bowl, combine all remaining ingredients except mushroom soup.
5. Toss until it is well mixed.
6. Spray a 12″x18″ piece of foil with non-stick spray.
7. Place ¼ of the vegetable mixture in the center of the foil.

8. Top with 1 beef patty.

9. Add 2 tablespoons of condensed mushroom soup on top of each patty.

10. Seal the foil packets well.

11. Place beef side up on a large baking sheet and bake 35-45 minutes or until potatoes and carrots are soft.

12. Serve and enjoy

CREAMY SALSA VERDE, CHICKEN, RICE, AND VEGGIES

Your family will love a tasty Mexican dinner—and you will love that it only takes 10 minutes to put together. Creamy salsa verde chicken with rice and veggies all cooked at once in a foil packet! No need to pre-cook the rice or chicken. This dish takes no more than 10 minutes to assemble and is bursting with delicious Mexican flavor.

PREP TIME: 10 minutes

COOK TIME: 40 minutes

TOTAL TIME: 50 minutes

Creamy Salsa Verde, Chicken, Rice With Veggies

Ingredients

- 1 cup of Instant white rice
- 1 ½ cups of water
- 2 (7 ounces each) large boneless skinless chicken breasts
- 1/2 teaspoon of each: cumin, garlic powder, salt and pepper
- 1 teaspoon of chili powder
- 1/8 teaspoon of paprika optional
- 1 ounce full fat cream cheese
- 6 tablespoons of salsa verde
- ½ cup of roasted corn
- ½ cup of black beans
- ½ cup of pepperjack cheese
- **Optional**: *roasted green chiles lime, cilantro, sour cream, red bell pepper*

Preparation

1. Preheat the oven to 400 degrees F.
2. Generously grease with cooking spray 2 large sheets of heavy duty tin foil.

3. Weigh your chicken to get (2) 7-ounce pieces.

4. 1 pound of or slice the pieces to ½ inch thickness.

5. Toss together the instant rice, water, and wait for 5 minutes.

6. In a bowl, toss together all of the seasonings: cumin, garlic powder, salt, pepper, chili powder, and paprika.

7. Dredge each chicken breast evenly in the seasonings (both sides).

8. Divide the rice and water mixture evenly among the 2 foil packets.

9. Place the seasoned chicken on top.

10. Slice the cream cheese into 4 equal pieces and place 2 pieces on top of each chicken breast.

11. Pour 3 tablespoons of salsa verde on top of each chicken breast.

12. Put ¼ cup of corn and ¼ cup of black beans next to each chicken breast.

13. If desired add a few pieces of thinly sliced red pepper to each packet.

14. Seal the packet allowing for expansion and make sure it is 100% sealed.

15. Bake for 30-50 minutes   or until the chicken is completely cooked through (registers 165 degrees F)

16. Mix everything around in your foil pack and top each with pepper jack cheese.

17. Add other optional toppings as desired.

18. **TO GRILL:** Preheat the grill to medium-high heat and allow it to heat for 10-15 minutes.

19. Place completely sealed foil packets on grill for 25-35 minutes (or until chicken registers 165 degrees F) flipping once in between at about 10-15 minutes.

GARLIC STEAK AND POTATO

A classic steak-and-potatoes dinner is even easier when you can just cook it in foil. Juicy and savory seasoned garlic steak and potato foil packs are the perfect baked or grilled 30-minute hearty, healthy meal.

PREP TIME: 10 minutes

COOK TIME: 20 minutes

TOTAL TIME: 30 minutes

Garlic Steak And Potato

Ingredients

- 2-2 ½ pounds of top sirloin steak, trimmed of fat and cut into 2 1/2-inch pieces
- 1 pound of baby yellow potatoes quartered
- 3 tablespoons of olive oil
- salt and pepper, to taste (you can use about 1 Teaspoon of salt and ¼ teaspoon of black pepper)
- 1 tablespoon of minced garlic
- ½ teaspoon of onion powder
- 1 teaspoon of dried oregano
- 1 teaspoon of dried parsley
- 1 teaspoon of dried thyme
- Fresh Thyme Or Parsley For Topping (Optional)

Preparation

1. In a large bowl, combine steak, potatoes, olive oil, salt and pepper, garlic, and seasonings and toss to combine.

2. Divide steak and potatoes between four 12x12 inch sheets of foil, then wrap the foil tightly around the contents to form your foil packs.

3. Grill over high heat for about 10 minutes on each side or until steak and potatoes are cooked through or bake at 425 degrees for about 20-25 minutes until cooked through to desired doneness.

4. Garnish with fresh thyme or parsley and serve immediately.

GARLIC SALMON IN FOIL PACKET

If you are cooking for a crowd, try this buttery salmon recipe. With little cooking Time (25 minutes!) and few dishes to wash, you will be able to spend more Time enjoying your party. This Garlic Lovers Salmon is easy to make on the grill or in the oven, it is cooked with the most heavenly lemon butter garlic sauce, and it is always a crowd favorite!

PREP TIME: 7 minutes

COOK TIME: 18 minutes

TOTAL TIME: 28 minutes

Garlic Salmon In Foil Packet

Ingredients

- 2 pound of side of salmon, boneless and skinless
- 4 tablespoons of butter
- 8 cloves garlic, peeled and roughly chopped
- ¼ cup of dry white wine
- 2 tablespoons of freshly-squeezed lemon juice, plus extra lemon wedges for serving
- Salt and pepper
- ¼ cup of chopped fresh Italian parsley
- ¼ cup of thinly-sliced green onions

Preparation

1. Heat oven to 375°F. Alternatively, heat a grill to medium heat.
2. Line a large baking dish with a large piece of aluminum foil.
3. In a small saucepan, heat the butter over medium-high heat until it melts.
4. Stir in the garlic and cook for 1-2 minutes until fragrant. (
5. Remove from heat and stir in the white wine and lemon juice.

6. Using a pastry brush, brush a tablespoons of the butter mixture on the foil until it is evenly covered.

7. Lay the salmon out on the foil.

8. Then pour the remainder of the butter-garlic mixture on top of the salmon and brush it around until it evenly covers the salmon.

9. Season the salmon evenly with a few generous pinches of salt and pepper.

10. Fold the sides of the aluminum foil up and over the top of the salmon until it is completely enclosed.

11. **To Cook In the Oven:** Bake for 14-15 minutes, or until the salmon is almost completely cooked through.

12. Remove the salmon from the oven and carefully open and pull back the aluminum foil so that the top of the fish is completely exposed.

13. Change the oven setting to broil, and then return the fish to the oven and broil for 3-4 minutes, or until the top of the salmon and the garlic are golden and the fish is cooked through. *(Keep a close eye on the salmon while broiling, though, to be sure that the garlic does not burn.)*

14. **To Cook On the Grill:** Carefully transfer the packet of salmon to the grill, and grill for 12-14 minutes, or until the salmon is almost completely cooked through.

15. Carefully open and pull back the aluminum foil so that the top of the fish is completely exposed.

16. Continue cooking for 3-4 minutes, or until the top of the salmon and the garlic are slightly golden and the fish is cooked through.

17. Remove salmon from the oven or grill.

18. Sprinkle the top of the salmon evenly with parsley and green onions, and serve immediately.

BBQ CHICKEN

Pack these barbecue chicken packets loaded with corn, peppers, and pineapple on your next family picnic. These fun, easy and tasty BBQ Chicken Foil Packs are the perfect Spring and Summer picnic, party or weeknight meals that the whole family will enjoy!

PREP TIME: 7 minutes

COOK TIME: 18 minutes

TOTAL TIME: 28 minutes

Bbq Chicken

Ingredients

- 2 diced Chicken breasts
- 1 cup of BBQ sauce, more for dopping
- 1 large baking potato, Diced
- 1 cup of corn
- ½ cup of diced red onion
- 1 red diced bell pepper
- 1 ½ cup of pineapple chunks

Preparation

1. Preheat grill or oven to 350.
2. In bowl a mix, your chicken and barbecue sauce.
3. In double lined or heavy-duty tin foil, add your potatoes, chicken, corn, onion, pepper and pineapple.
4. Fold your tin foil over the BBQ Chicken and then roll up on ends.
5. Place on baking sheet or directly on grill and cook for about 40-50 minutes or until potatoes are soft.
6. Let cool slightly and serve.

Very Good!

PARMESAN CHICKEN

Put your summer tomatoes to use in this chicken dinner that is topped with melted mozzarella cheese. Chicken Parmesan Foil Packets are a super easy summer meal! You are going to love how simple both the preparation and the cleanup are, and to top it off, they are delicious!

PREP TIME: 15 minutes

COOK TIME: 20 minutes

TOTAL TIME: 35 minutes

Parmesan Chicken

Ingredients

- 4 boneless, skinless chicken breasts
- 3 cups of pasta sauce
- 2 sliced zucchini
- ½ cup of parmesan cheese shredded
- 1 cup of mozzarella cheese shredded
- 1 teaspoon of garlic powder
- 1 teaspoon of Italian seasoning sprinkle
- Salt & pepper to taste
- ¼ cup of olive oil
- Spaghetti cooked
- Parsley freshly chopped

Preparation

1. Preheat grill to medium heat.
2. Spray four 12x18 inch foil pieces with cooking spray.
3. Divide zucchini over the four pieces of foil.
4. Sprinkle with salt, pepper and italian seasoning to taste and 2 tablespoons of parmesan cheese.
5. Add 1/3 cup of pasta sauce on top of the zucchini.

6. Place a chicken breast on top of the sauce.

7. Drizzle each chicken breast with olive oil then sprinkle with garlic powder, Italian seasoning, salt and pepper.

8. Seal each packet.

9. Place on heated grill with the chicken side down.

10. Grill for 8 minutes.

11. Flip each packet and continue to grill for another 8-10 minutes or until juice run clear and chicken reaches 165 degrees.

12. Open each packet by slicing with a knife.

13. Sprinkle ¼ cup of mozzarella cheese on each chicken breast and heat to melt.

14. If desired, cook pasta according to package PREPARATION and heat remaining sauce.

15. Remove the chicken and zucchini from each packet and place on top of the pasta.

16. Pour any extra sauce from the packet on top as well.

17. Sprinkle with freshly grated parmesan and garnish with fresh parsley.

18. Serve and enjoy.

CILANTRO LIME SHRIMP WITH CAULIFLOWER RICE

Looking for an easy low-carb dinner option? This recipe calls for cauliflower instead of white rice, but still packs plenty of protein to keep you full and satisfied. Cilantro Lime Shrimp and Cauliflower Rice Foil Packs are a flavorful easy dinner you cannot pass by! Shrimp and veggies are boasting of bright fresh Mexican flavors and it is a recipe that is set to impress everyone.

PREP TIME: 20 minutes

COOK TIME: 10 minutes

TOTAL TIME: 30 minutes

Cilantro Lime Shrimp With Cauliflower Rice

Ingredients

- 1 medium-large head of cauliflower (or 4 cups of Frozen cauliflower rice thawed)
- 1 ¼ pound of peeled and deveined large (21/25) shrimp
- 1 (14 ounces) can of black beans, drained and rinsed well
- 1 ear corn, shucked and kernels cut from cob, (or 1 cup of Frozen corn, thawed)
- 1 (4 ounces) can of diced mild green chilies, drained
- ½ cup of sliced green onions, white and light green portion
- 1 tablespoon of minced garlic
- 2 ½ tablespoon of olive oil
- 1 teaspoon of lime zest
- 2 tablespoon of fresh lime juice
- 1 teaspoon of grinded cumin
- Salt and freshly grinded black pepper
- 1/3 cup of chopped cilantro
- 1 small sliced avocado

Preparation

1. Preheat a gas grill over moderately high heat to about 450 - 475 degrees.

2. Cut cauliflower florets from head, leaving behind as much stem as possible.

3. Working in 2 or 3 batches, pulse florets in a food processor until cauliflower is finely chopped (it should look similar to couscous).

4. Measure out 4 cups of and transfer to a large bowl.

5. Add shrimp to bowl along with black beans, corn, green chilies, green onions, garlic, olive oil, lime zest, limejuice, and cumin. Season with salt and pepper (about 1 Teaspoon of salt 1/4 Teaspoon of pepper) then toss gently to evenly coat.

6. Cut 4 sheets of 15 by 12-inch heavy duty aluminum foil.

7. Lay the sheets individually on a flat surface.

8. Divide shrimp mixture evenly among foil sheets, while placing each mound in the center of the foil.

9. Bring the sides of foil inward then fold together twice and to seal, then fold ends up.

10. Grill the packets until shrimp has cooked through (it should appear pink in color), for about 9 - 11 minutes.

11. Carefully open each packet and toss in cilantro.

12. Serve warm with avocado slices.

SHRIMP BOIL

Nothing says summer quite like a low-country boil and this version is ready in just 15 minutes. Easy, make-ahead foil packets packed with shrimp, sausage, corn and potatoes. It is a full meal with zero clean up!

PREP TIME: 10 minutes

COOK TIME: 15 minutes

TOTAL TIME: 25 minutes

Shrimp Boil

Ingredients

- 1 ½ pounds of peeled and deveined large shrimp
- 1 (12.8-ounce) package of thinly sliced smoked andouille sausage
- 2 ears corn, each cut crosswise into 4 pieces
- 1 pound of baby red potatoes, halved
- 2 tablespoons of olive oil
- 4 teaspoons of cajun seasoning
- Kosher salt and freshly grinded black pepper, to taste
- 2 tablespoons of chopped fresh parsley leaves

Preparation

1. Preheat a gas or charcoal grill over high heat.
2. Cut four sheets of foil, about 12-inches long.
3. Divide the shrimp, sausage, corn and potatoes into 4 equal portions and add to the center of each foil in a single layer.
4. Fold up all 4 sides of each foil packet.
5. Add olive oil, cajun seasoning, salt and pepper, to taste; gently toss to combine.

6. Fold the sides of the foil over the shrimp, covering completely and sealing the packets closed.

7. Place foil packets on the grill and cook until just cooked through, about 12-15 minutes.

8. Served immediately, garnished with parsley, if desired.

GRILLED HERB CRUSTED POTATOES AND

PORK SOFTLOIN

Yes, you can make an entire pork Softloin in a foil pack. Surround the pork with red potatoes, and then top with with rosemary, sage, and parmesan.

PREP TIME: 10 minutes

COOK TIME: 15 minutes

TOTAL TIME: 25 minutes

Grilled Herb Crusted Potatoes And Pork Softloin

Ingredients

- 1 ½ pounds of peeled and deveined large shrimp
- 1 (12.8-ounce) package of thinly sliced smoked andouille sausage
- 2 ears corn, each cut crosswise into 4 pieces
- 1 pound of baby red potatoes, halved
- 2 tablespoons of olive oil
- 4 teaspoons of cajun seasoning
- Kosher salt and freshly grinded black pepper, to taste
- 2 tablespoons of chopped fresh parsley leaves

Preparation

1. Heat a grill to medium heat.
2. In a mixing bowl, combine the chopped potatoes with the olive oil, herbs, parmesan, salt and pepper.
3. Stir until well combined and completely covered.
4. Grab a large section of aluminum foil and spray well with cooking spray.

5. Lay the Smithfield Golden Rotisserie Marinated Fresh Pork Softloin in the center of the foil and line the potatoes along each side.

6. Carefully fold up the foil on each side and create a packet.

7. Place the packet seam side up on the grill and cook for 30 minutes.

8. Remove from grill and very carefully open (the steam will be hot!

9. Garnish with additional herbs and parmesan if desired.

10. Please note if your pork loin is larger than one Pound of your cooking time will increase.

CHICKEN MILANO

This Italian dish is perfect for the nights you do not want to deal with a ton of clean up. Healthy and fast, this Chicken Milano Foil Packet

Recipe is great for a weeknight. The chicken is moist and flavorful, and cleanup is a breeze!

PREP TIME: 15 minutes

COOK TIME: 20 minutes

TOTAL TIME: 35 minutes

Chicken Milano

Ingredients

- 2 boneless, skinless chicken breasts (about 8–10 ounces of each)
- ¼ cup of prepared Italian dressing (light or reduced calorie works)
- 8 Ounces of fresh mushrooms, sliced
- ¼ cup of fresh basil, plus more for topping
- ¼ cup of julienned sun-dried tomatoes (dried, not in oil)
- ¼ cup of freshly grated Parmesan cheese

Preparation

1. Preheat the oven to 450°F.
2. Butterfly each of the chicken breasts open and cut into two thinner pieces so you have 4 pieces of chicken.
3. Cut 4 large pieces of heavy-duty foil.
4. Place one piece of chicken in the center of each piece of foil.
5. Top with 1 tablespoon of Italian dressing, ¼ of the mushrooms, ¼ of the basil, and 1/4 of the tomatoes.
6. Season with salt and pepper.
7. Bring up 2 sides of the foil and seal.

8. Fold the opposite edges to form a packet.

9. There should be some room in the package for heat circulation.

10. Repeat with the remaining ingredients.

11. Place the foil packets on a baking sheet, and place in the oven.

12. Bake for 15-20 minutes, or until the juice of the chicken is no longer pink, and when a thermometer inserted in the thickest part of the breast registers 165ºF.

13. Fold back the foil of each packet and top with the Parmesan cheese.

14. Add more basil, if desired.

CHESSY RANCH CHICKEN POTATO

Cheesy Ranch Chicken Potato Foil Packets are a campfire favorite. This simple and comforting dinner will keep your campers happy all summer!

PREP TIME: 10 minutes

COOK TIME: 20 minutes

TOTAL TIME: 30 minutes

Chessy Ranch Chicken Potato

Ingredients

- 1 pound of boneless skinless chicken breast
- 1 pound of golden new potatoes
- 1 large red bell pepper
- 1 small red onion
- 2 tablespoons of olive oil
- 1 packet ranch dip seasoning
- 8 slices Land O Lakes White Deli American (3/4 ounce)
- 2 tablespoons of chopped parsley
- Salt and pepper

Preparation

1. Slice the potatoes into 1/3-inch slices.
2. Cut the bell pepper and peeled onion into 1-inch pieces.
3. Place the chopped veggies in a bowl.
4. Mix in the olive oil and the ranch-seasoning packet.
5. Toss to coat
6. Lay four 14x18-inch pieces of foil out on the counter.
7. Divide the vegetables evenly between the foil pieces, piling them in the middle of each piece.

8. Chop the chicken into 1-inch chunks.

9. Season liberally with salt and pepper.

10. Then pile the chicken pieces evenly on top of the veggie piles.

11. Lift the long ends of the foil over each chicken and vegetable stack and neatly fold them together at least three Times so they stay secure.

12. Then fold the shorter ends toward the center at least three Times each, on both sides.

13. The packets should be tightly secured on all sides.

14. Refrigerate or place in an ice chest until ready to grill.

15. When ready to cook, preheat a grill to high heat, between 500-600 degrees.

16. Once hot, place the packets on the grill and cook for 20 minutes.

17. Remove the foil packets with tongs and carefully open them up.

18. Then place two slices of Land O Lakes White Deli American and a sprinkle of chopped parsley over each packet.

19. Set them back on the grill for 1-2 minutes, just long enough for the cheese to melt.

20. Serve warm!

LEMON BAKED COD WITH ASPARAGUS

All it takes is a little salt, pepper, olive oil, and breadcrumbs to make this fish taste delicious. Dinner does not get easier or healthier than this! Baked lemon cod and asparagus are roasted together in a foil packet. Super flavorful dinner with easy cleanup.

PREP TIME: 10 minutes

COOK TIME: 16 minutes

TOTAL TIME: 26 minutes

Lemon Baked Cod With Asparagus

Ingredients

- 12 ounces cod, fresh or dethawed, at room temperature
- 1 pound of asparagus, washed and trimmed
- 2.5 medium lemons, sliced into rounds
- ½ medium yellow onion, sliced into rounds/rings
- 2 tablespoon of olive oil
- ½ tablespoon of garlic salt
- ½ tablespoon of lemon pepper
- ½ tablespoon of Schnucks Italian Bread Crumbs

Preparation

1. Preheat oven to 425 degrees.
2. Place large foil sheet on baking tray.
3. Spray with cooking coil.
4. Place slices of one lemon, and half of the onion slices on the foil sheet.
5. Top lemon and onion with asparagus, then another layer of lemon and onion.

6. Top with cod. Sprinkle everything with olive oil, garlic salt and lemon pepper. Squeeze juice of 1/2 lemon over top. Sprinkle bread crumbs over cod.

7. Roast for 13-15 minutes, until cod starts to flake and asparagus is crisp-Soft.

8. **Optional:** Broil on top rack for 1 minute to brown bread crumbs.

SWEET POTATO TACOS

This kind of Sweet Potato Tacos recipes made in a Foil is packed with flavorful tacos and delicious sweet potatoes filling bake in total harmony since the little envelope captures all the streams and creates perfect atmosphere for the flavors to blend and cook together. This recipe is an amazing foil packet recipe that is nutritious, filling, and crazy delicious.

PREP TIME: 20 minutes

COOK TIME: 38 minutes

TOTAL TIME: 58 minutes

Sweet Potato Tacos

Ingredients

- 2 pounds of grinded turkey or beef
- 1 teaspoon of salt
- ½ teaspoon of black pepper
- ½ cup of finely chopped onion
- ½ tablespoon of chili powder
- 1 teaspoon of grinded cumin
- 2 teaspoons of grinded coriander
- 16 ounces tomato sauce
- 1 jalapeño, seeded, membranes removed and finely chopped
- 1/3 cup of water
- 2 cups of chopped fresh spinach
- 2 cans (15-ounces each) beans (black, pinto, white), rinsed and drained
- 4 medium sweet potatoes, peeled and chopped small (1/2-inch pieces)
- **Garnishes:**
- Shredded Cheese, Sour Cream, Avocados Or Guacamole, Salsa, Olives, Cilantro

Preparation

1. Preheat the oven to 425 degrees F.

2. In a large 12-inch nonstick skillet over medium heat, add the grinded meat, salt, pepper, and onion.

3. Cook, while breaking the meat into small pieces, until the meat is cooked through.

4. Drain any excess grease.

5. Add the chili powder, cumin, coriander, tomato sauce and jalapeño (if using).

6. Cook over medium heat for 2-3 minutes, stirring often. Stir in the water, spinach and beans and simmer for 4-5 minutes.

7. Remove from the heat.

8. Lightly grease the center of 6-8 foil pieces, each about 12-inches long.

9. Place about 1 cup of sweet potato chunks in the center of each piece of foil arranging them into somewhat of a single layer; sprinkle with salt and pepper

10. Add a heaping ½ cup of the meat mixture on top.

11. Bring the long sides of foil together over the filling and fold tightly down.

12. Fold and crimp each edge until tightly sealed and a little packet is formed.

13. Repeat with all the pieces of foil and ingredients.

14. Place the foil packets in a single layer on a large, rimmed baking sheet and bake for 20-25 minutes until the potatoes are soft.

15. Carefully open the foil packets and serve with taco toppings and garnishes of your choice.

CONCLUSION

Using aluminum foil to package your food helps to seal in the odor without having to open your fridge and be stopped dead in your tracks because of an unbearable smell. Just be sure to tightly pinch the foil to the sides of the container so no air can go in or come out. Foil wrapping is ideal for anyone who is storing food that will be reheating it in the near future. Since aluminum foil can withstand high temperatures, it makes this food packing material the best tool for the job.

Aluminum foil is impervious to moisture, light, bacteria and all gases. Because of its ability to block out bacteria and moisture especially, it helps the food last longer than if it were wrapped in plastic.

The ease of packaging your food with aluminum foil is what makes it the most ideal house hold and food industry item. It forms easily around any shape and takes just a few seconds to complete the packaging process.